Excel 2011 for Mac Pivot Tables

Tim Hill

Questing Vole Press

Excel 2011 for Mac Pivot Tables (Tech 102)
by Tim Hill

Editor: Kevin Debenjak
Proofreader: Janet Ott
Compositor: Kim Frees
Cover Illustrator: Rayne Beaudoin
Cover: Questing Vole Press

Contents

1

Pivot Table Basics

You can use Excel's **pivot tables** to quickly create concise, flexible summaries of long lists of raw values, without having to write new formulas, copy and paste cells, or reorganize rows and columns. Pivot tables are **dynamic**: if you create a pivot table from, say, census data, then you can drag your mouse to rearrange the table so that it summarizes any variables of interest—age, gender, location, education, income, and so on. Rearranging a pivot table by swapping or moving rows and columns is called **pivoting**: turning the same information to view it at different angles. The jargon associated with pivot tables ("*n*-dimensional cross tabulations") makes them look complex, but they're really no more than an easy way to build flexible summary tables.

Excel offers other features for analyzing large amounts of data—including outlines, automatic subtotals, and statistical functions—but if you're working with hundreds (or hundreds of thousands) of rows, then pivot tables are the best way to look at the same information in different ways, summarize data on the fly, and spot trends and relationships.

Downloading the Sample Workbook

To create a pivot table, you need a long list of raw data values to summarize. (A short list works too but doesn't show the real power of pivot tables.) To follow along with the examples in this book, download the Excel workbook **orders11.xlsx** from *questingvolepress.com*.

In orders11.xlsx, the worksheet named Source Data contains a list of 2155 records (rows) from grocery-item orders.

Order ID	Product	Category	Unit Price	Quantity	Customer	Ship City	Ship Country	Order Date
10248	Singaporean Hokkien Fried Mee	Grains/Cereals	9.8	10	Vins et alcools Chevalier	Reims	France	04-Aug-94
10248	Mozzarella di Giovanni	Dairy Products	34.8	5	Vins et alcools Chevalier	Reims	France	04-Aug-94
10248	Queso Cabrales	Dairy Products	14	12	Vins et alcools Chevalier	Reims	France	04-Aug-94
10249	Tofu	Produce	18.6	9	Toms Spezialitäten	Münster	Germany	05-Aug-94
10249	Manjimup Dried Apples	Produce	42.4	40	Toms Spezialitäten	Münster	Germany	05-Aug-94
10250	Louisiana Fiery Hot Pepper Sauce	Condiments	16.8	15	Hanari Carnes	Rio de Janeiro	Brazil	08-Aug-94
10250	Jack's New England Clam Chowder	Seafood	7.7	10	Hanari Carnes	Rio de Janeiro	Brazil	08-Aug-94
10250	Manjimup Dried Apples	Produce	42.4	35	Hanari Carnes	Rio de Janeiro	Brazil	08-Aug-94
10251	Louisiana Fiery Hot Pepper Sauce	Condiments	16.8	20	Victuailles en stock	Lyon	France	08-Aug-94
10251	Gustaf's Knäckebröd	Grains/Cereals	16.8	6	Victuailles en stock	Lyon	France	08-Aug-94
10251	Ravioli Angelo	Grains/Cereals	15.6	15	Victuailles en stock	Lyon	France	08-Aug-94
10252	Sir Rodney's Marmalade	Confections	64.8	40	Suprêmes délices	Charleroi	Belgium	09-Aug-94
10252	Geitost	Dairy Products	2	25	Suprêmes délices	Charleroi	Belgium	09-Aug-94
10252	Camembert Pierrot	Dairy Products	27.2	40	Suprêmes délices	Charleroi	Belgium	09-Aug-94
10253	Maxilaku	Confections	16	40	Hanari Carnes	Rio de Janeiro	Brazil	10-Aug-94
10253	Chartreuse verte	Beverages	14.4	42	Hanari Carnes	Rio de Janeiro	Brazil	10-Aug-94
10253	Gorgonzola Telino	Dairy Products	10	20	Hanari Carnes	Rio de Janeiro	Brazil	10-Aug-94
10254	Pâté chinois	Meat/Poultry	19.2	21	Chop-suey Chinese	Bern	Switzerland	11-Aug-94
10254	Longlife Tofu	Produce	8	21	Chop-suey Chinese	Bern	Switzerland	11-Aug-94

Source Data

Data Requirements for Pivot Tables

Pivot tables let you make comparisons and answer specific questions. To work well with pivot tables, a data list needs to meet the following criteria.

At least one column has duplicate values

Pivot tables are used to divide a list into logical **levels** (categories) and calculate statistics for each level. In the sample orders list, the column Customer, for example, has multiple records with the same value (denoting repeat customers). You can summarize the items ordered by each customer where each distinct customer is one level. In real-life data, the number of distinct values in a categorical column ranges from a few (gender or marital status, for example) to a few hundred (geographic location or part number); beyond a few hundred distinct values, analysis becomes unwieldy unless you group (Chapter 3) or filter (Chapter 5) categories.

At least one column has numerical values

Numerical values are used to calculate statistics (sum, count, average, maximum, percentage, custom formula, and more) for each column and level of interest. For non-numerical columns, the only statistics that you can calculate are frequency tabulations (page 54): counts of the number of levels (distinct values) in the column. For details about calculating statistics, see Chapter 4.

Sample Workbook Columns

The orders list in the sample workbook (page 1) contains the following columns.

Order ID

> Categorical. Identifies an order uniquely. An order for multiple products spans multiple rows. Order 10248, for example, spans rows 2, 3, and 4 (one product per row). Though the order IDs are numbers (10248, 10249,...), this column is actually categorical because it makes no sense to do mathematical operations on its values (summing IDs is meaningless, for example).

Product

> Categorical. The brand name of the ordered product (Jack's New England Clam Chowder, Manjimup Dried Apples, and so on).

Category

> Categorical. The type of the ordered product (Seafood, Produce, and so on).

Unit Price

> Numerical. The selling price of a single unit of the ordered product.

Quantity

> Numerical. The number of units of the product sold in the order.

Customer

> Categorical. The name of the buyer.

Ship City

> Categorical. The city (in Ship Country) where the order was shipped.

Ship Country

> Categorical. The country where the order was shipped.

Order Date

> Categorical. The date that the order was placed.

Creating Pivot Tables

To create a new pivot table, you run the Create PivotTable wizard, which lets you select the data to summarize and position the pivot table on a worksheet. You can then structure the pivot table and organize and filter your data however you like.

To create a pivot table:

1   Select the range of cells (including column titles) that you want to use for the pivot table. Alternatively, select a single cell in the range and Excel will expand the range automatically; if Excel misidentifies the range, you can fix it in the next step.

It's actually preferable to use a *table* (Tables tab > Table Options group > New arrow > Insert Table with Headers, or press Ctrl+T) instead of selecting a range of cells. That way, Excel automatically accounts for any new rows that you add to the source data when you refresh the pivot table (page 13). If you use a range instead of a table, then you must redefine the data source if you add new rows to the end of the range (PivotTable tab > Data group > Change Source).

2   Choose Data tab > Analysis group > PivotTable arrow > Create Manual PivotTable.

Alternatively, if you're creating a pivot table for a table that you defined with Tables tab > Table Options group > New, then you can click anywhere inside the table and then choose Tables tab > Tools group > Summarize with PivotTable.

The Create PivotTable dialog box opens. Excel automatically chooses "Use a table or a range in this workbook", with the table name or cell range that you selected.

3 Select "New worksheet" to create a new worksheet for the pivot table (typically the best option).

Alternatively, choose "Existing worksheet" to insert the pivot table on a worksheet that's already in your workbook. Specify the cell reference for the top-left corner of the pivot table. Excel overwrites any values in the target cells when it creates the pivot table.

In general, it's safest to place a pivot table on its own new worksheet. If you restructure the pivot table, it can grow to overwrite other values on the sheet (Excel warns you before overwriting existing data).

4 Click OK.

Excel inserts the new pivot table. The pivot table appears as an empty placeholder until you define the rows, columns, and values to use to summarize the source data. When you select a cell inside the pivot table, Excel displays the PivotTable Builder on the right, which lists all the columns in the source data.

If you chose to create a new worksheet, Excel gives the sheet a generic name (Sheet2 or whatever) and then places it before the worksheet that contains the source data. You can rename the new worksheet (double-click its worksheet tab) and then drag the tab left or right to reposition the worksheet.

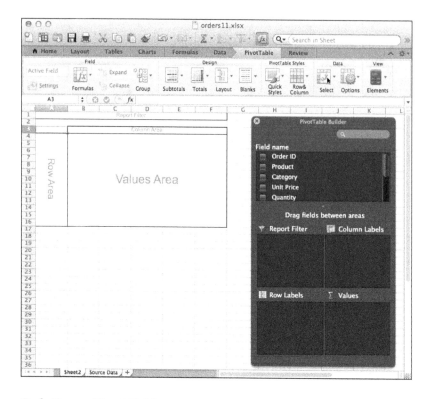

Deleting a Pivot Table

A pivot table is a monolithic grid, meaning deletion is all-or-nothing. Excel won't let you insert or delete individual cells, rows, or columns in a pivot table.

To delete a pivot table:

1   Select the entire pivot table.

To select the entire pivot table, drag to select all the pivot table's cells (including headers) or right-click any cell in the pivot table and then choose Select > Entire Table. Alternatively, click anywhere in the pivot table and then choose PivotTable tab > Data group > Select > Entire Table.

2   Choose Edit > Clear > All.

Laying Out Pivot Tables

To lay out a pivot table, you use the **PivotTable Builder**. Drag columns, called **fields**, from the "Field name" list into any of the four boxes underneath. You can also select the checkbox next to a field; Excel will place it in a box depending on the field's data type (if Excel guesses wrong, drag the field to the correct box). Excel updates the pivot table dynamically as you add, rearrange, or remove fields.

The PivotTable Builder appears when you select any cell in a pivot table. If it doesn't appear, choose PivotTable tab > View group > Builder.

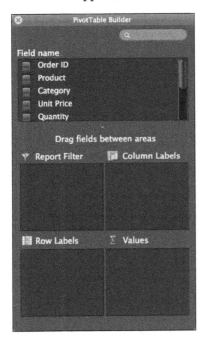

A pivot table has four areas:

Values

> These fields are the numerical values for which you want to display sums, averages, counts, and other statistics. For example, you can drag the Unit Price field here to calculate price statistics. (If you drag a non-numerical field to Values, only counts are calculated.) For details, see Chapter 4.

Row Labels

These fields group the data into levels, one level per row. For example, you can drag the Category field here to show product categories (Beverages, Condiments, and so on).

Column Labels

These fields also create levels, one level per column. You can use both Row Labels and Column Labels to divide your data in multiple ways in the same pivot table. Drag Ship Country to Row Labels, Category to Column Labels, and Quantity to Values, for example. The pivot table divides sales figures into rows by country and columns by product category, answering the question, "Which types of products sell best in each country?".

Report Filter

These fields limit the data displayed in the pivot table. For example, to show a breakdown of U.S.-only sales by product category, drag Ship Country to Report Filter and then configure the filter to show only "USA" values. For details, see "Report Filters" on page 46.

Rearranging (Pivoting) a Pivot Table

In the PivotTable Builder, you can remove or move fields at any time to rearrange (pivot) the pivot table.

To remove a field from a pivot table:

- Drag the field from any box out of the PivotTable Builder (the mouse pointer changes to a circle-slash symbol as you drag).

  or

  Clear the checkbox next to the field name in the field list.

To move a field from one area to another:

- Drag the field from one box to another.

Row or Column Label?

Choosing whether a field appears as a row or column label is a matter of formatting and readability (either way, the same data are displayed). Fields with long category names or many distinct values typically work better as row labels (as column labels, they stretch or proliferate columns). For example, the Product field works best as a row label; as a column label, the pivot table would be 77 columns wide (Alice Mutton, Aniseed Syrup,..., Zaanse koeken) and hard to read and print.

Moving a Pivot Table

You can move a pivot table to a new worksheet or an existing one. Select any cell in the pivot table and then choose PivotTable tab > Data group > Move.

PivotTable Options

You can change the most common pivot-table settings by using the ribbon and the PivotTable Builder, but you can find many others in the PivotTable Options dialog box. To open it, right-click any cell in the pivot table and then choose PivotTable Options (or choose PivotTable tab > Data group > Options). Settings made in this dialog box apply to only the active pivot table.

Layout Examples

The following example creates a summary that compares products and shipping locations. The result is a **two-dimensional** pivot table. Most pivot tables seen in practice are two-dimensional, meaning that they summarize two different fields.

Tip: If you're using the sample workbook (page 1) to follow along, the look of your pivot tables depends on which report layout (compact, outline, or tabular form) you choose. For details, see "Formatting Pivot Tables" on page 14.

To compare products and shipping locations:

1   If necessary, create a new pivot table (page 4).

2   In the PivotTable Builder, drag the Product field to the Row Labels box underneath.

Excel fills in all the product names from the source data from top to bottom (in alphabetical order), one product per row.

3   Drag the Ship Country field to the Column Labels box.

Excel fills in all the country names from the source data from left to right (in alphabetical order), one country per column.

4   Drag the Quantity field to the Values box.

This step chooses which data to examine. Excel fills the pivot table with the numbers of products that were ordered by customers in various countries. The default calculation for pivot tables is the sum of each field in the Values box (note the label "Sum of Quantity" in the Values box). In this example, each value is the total number of units of a specific product shipped to a specific country.

Pivot tables also calculate subtotals and grand totals. To see them, scroll to rightmost or bottommost end of the pivot table. The grand total is in the bottom-right corner.

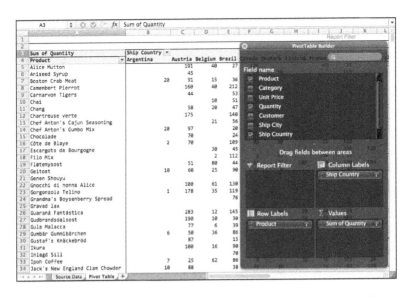

You can also *nest* fields by placing them together in the Row Labels or Column Labels box. For example, starting with an empty pivot table, drag Product to the Row Labels box, drag Ship Country to the same box (placing it under Product), and then drag Quantity to the Values box. The order of fields within a box determines their nesting order in the pivot table (here, Ship Country is nested within Product). For details, see Chapter 2.

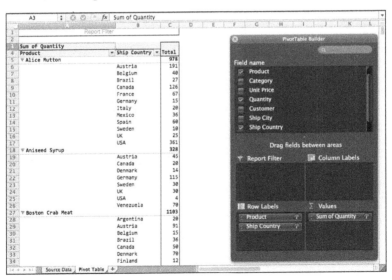

A **one-dimensional** pivot table has a single field in either the Column Labels or Row Labels box (but not both). For example, starting with an empty pivot table, drag Product to the Row Labels box and then drag Quantity to the Values box. The resulting pivot table simply totals the number of units sold by product.

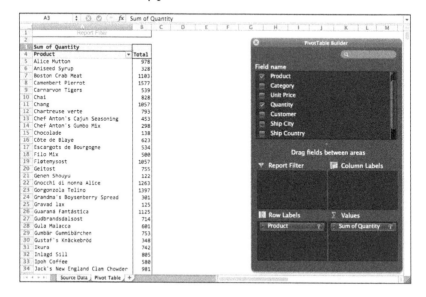

Refreshing Pivot Tables

Unlike formulas, charts, and most other elements in Excel, pivot tables don't auto-update when the underlying data change. If you change the source data, the pivot table can show out-of-date totals. A **refresh** makes Excel scan the source data and recalculate the pivot table.

To refresh a pivot table manually:

- Right-click the pivot table and then choose Refresh Data.

  or

  Select any cell in the pivot table and then choose PivotTable tab > Data group > Refresh button > Refresh (or click Refresh All to refresh all pivot tables in the workbook). If the Refresh button isn't visible, click the Options button instead.

To autorefresh a pivot table when you open a workbook:

- Select any cell in the pivot table and then choose PivotTable tab > Data group > Options > Data pane > select "Refresh data when opening file".

Tip: A refresh can take a long time depending on the amount of source data, the complexity of the pivot table, the speed of your computer, and other factors. After starting a refresh, you can cancel it at any time by choosing Cancel Refresh from the Refresh menu.

Autoformatting on Refresh

If a pivot table becomes misformatted when you refresh it, select the "AutoFit column widths on update" and "Preserve cell formatting on update" checkboxes on the Layout pane in the PivotTable Options dialog box (PivotTable tab > Data group > Options).

Formatting Pivot Tables

When you select a cell in a pivot table, the ribbon sprouts a PivotTable tab. In this tab, you can use the Design group and the PivotTable Styles group to change the appearance of pivot tables.

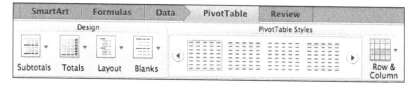

Subtotals

> Show subtotals at the top or bottom of each level. This setting applies only if fields are nested (Chapter 2); that is, the Row Labels or Column Labels box contains more than one field.

Totals

> Show or hide the grand totals at the end of each row or column.

Layout

> By default, pivot tables are shown in **compact form**: all row labels are merged into a single column, and each column just wide enough to fit that column's widest entry. In **outline form**, each row label gets its own column, and each column is as wide as the widest column in the whole pivot table (which occupies much more space). **Tabular form** is like outline form but shows subtotals (extra rows) at the bottom of each level or group. In compact form, you can control how far row levels are indented: choose PivotTable tab > Data group > Options > Layout pane > "In compact form, indent row labels".

Blanks

Show or hide blank lines between levels or groups. This option applies only if the Row Labels section has more than one field.

Quick Styles/Style Gallery

Click the Quick Styles button, or hover the pointer over the style gallery and then click the down arrow that appears. Click a style to change the colors and shading of the pivot table. Scroll up or down the list to see all available styles. To create a custom style, click "New PivotTable Style".

Row & Column

If you don't want to apply the style formatting to headers, clear Row Headers or Column Headers. If you don't want shading to alternate from one row or column to the next, clear Banded Rows or Banded Columns.

Tip: To show or hide field headers for rows and columns, choose PivotTable tab > View group > Headers.

Showing a Value's Source Data

If you spot a trend, unexpected relationship, or an outlier (suspicious observation) in a pivot table, you can easily "drill down" to see exactly how the value was calculated. To do so, double-click any value cell in a pivot table. Excel creates a new worksheet containing copies of only the records that were used to calculate that cell's value. This method is superior to the tedious alternative: switching to the worksheet that contains the original source data and then searching for the corresponding records.

The following pivot table shows how product categories (rows) perform in each country (columns). Double-click cell B5…

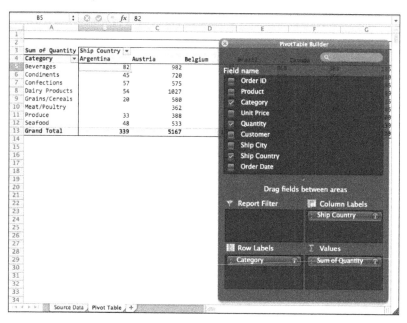

...and Excel adds a worksheet containing copies of the seven records whose Quantity values were summed to produce Argentine beverage sales.

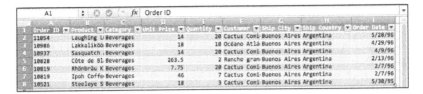

	A	B	C	D	E	F	G	H	I
1	Order ID	Product	Category	Unit Price	Quantity	Customer	Ship City	Ship Country	Order Date
2	11054	Laughing L	Beverages	14	28	Cactus Comi	Buenos Aires	Argentina	5/28/96
3	10986	Lakkaliköö	Beverages	18	18	Océano Atlá	Buenos Aires	Argentina	4/29/96
4	10937	Sasquatch	Beverages	14	28	Cactus Comi	Buenos Aires	Argentina	4/9/96
5	10828	Côte de Bl	Beverages	263.5	2	Rancho gran	Buenos Aires	Argentina	2/13/96
6	10819	Rhönbräu K	Beverages	7.75	28	Cactus Comi	Buenos Aires	Argentina	2/7/96
7	10819	Ipoh Coffe	Beverages	46	7	Cactus Comi	Buenos Aires	Argentina	2/7/96
8	10521	Steeleye S	Beverages	18	3	Cactus Comi	Buenos Aires	Argentina	5/30/95

After you finish examining the data, you can delete the worksheet that contains the copied records (right-click the worksheet tab at the bottom of the window and then choose Delete). The original source data aren't touched when you delete the copy.

If you spot an error in the copied records, you must flip to the original source data to fix it. Obvious, yes, but it's easy to absentmindedly change the *copied* records and then wonder why the refreshed pivot table doesn't change.

Changing a Pivot Table's Source Data

If you add rows to the bottom of a range of source data, you can redefine the pivot table's source data to include those rows. Select any cell in the pivot table and then choose PivotTable tab > Data group > Change Source.

Tip: If the source data are in an Excel table (Tables tab > Table Options group > New), then you don't have to change the range—newly added rows are displayed automatically when you refresh the pivot table.

2

Nesting Fields

You've already seen examples of one- and two-dimensional pivot tables (page 10), but Excel doesn't limit the number of fields in a pivot table.

To add additional (nested) fields to a pivot table:

1   Select any cell in the pivot table.

Excel shows the PivotTable Builder.

2   In the PivotTable Builder, drag fields from the "Field name" list to the Row Labels or Column Labels boxes underneath.

Each time you add a new field, Excel subdivides, or **nests**, the current fields. The order of fields within a box determines their nesting order in the pivot table.

Consider a pivot table with the settings:

Row Labels: Product, Ship Country
Column Labels: <empty>
Values: Quantity (summarized by Sum)
Report Filter: <empty>

Each row in this pivot table shows the total units of a specific product shipped to a specific country.

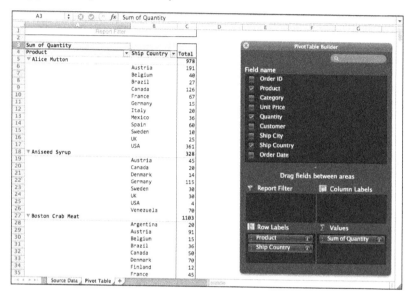

Excessive nesting can make a pivot table uninformative or unwieldy. If the number of rows in a pivot table is close to the number of rows in the underlying source data, then that pivot table isn't actually a summary. Another sign of an overnested pivot table is an excessive number of empty cells (wasted space).

Consider a pivot table with the settings:

Row Labels: Category, Order Date
Column Labels: Ship Country
Values: Quantity (summarized by Sum)
Report Filter: <empty>

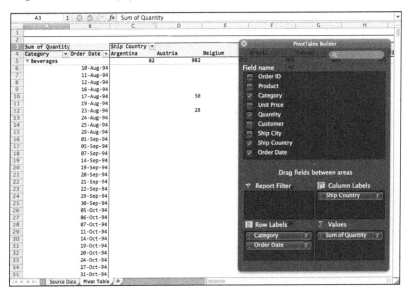

The rows in this pivot table are grouped by category and subdivided by order date. At 1605 rows (not counting subtotals or blank values), this pivot table isn't much smaller than the source data (2155 rows). The problem is that few orders fall on the same date. And when they do, they're usually for different product categories. Consequently, many rows show results for only a single order, rather than true totals. This pivot table is **sparse** (contains many empty cells) because each row is further broken up into columns by country.

Nesting works best for closely related fields, such as Category and Product (each product falls in one category):

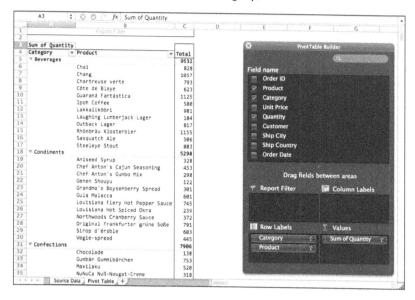

Or Ship Country and Ship City (each city is located in one country):

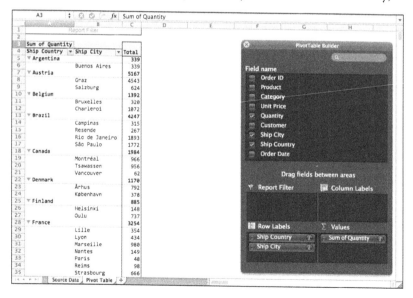

Make sure that you place the fields in the correct order in the Labels box; otherwise, you'll get silly results. Consider a pivot table with the settings:

Row Labels: Product, Category
Column Labels: <empty>
Values: Quantity (summarized by Sum)
Report Filter: <empty>

This pivot table groups the records by product and then subdivides the products by category, resulting in an unhelpful pivot table where each group contains a single subgroup (because each product falls in only one category). To fix this pivot table, swap the row labels.

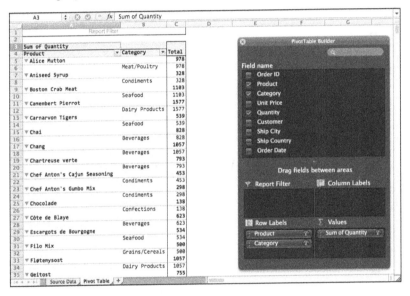

To reorder fields in a pivot table:

1 Select any cell in the pivot table.

Excel shows the PivotTable Builder.

2 In the PivotTable Builder, drag fields up or down within a box.

Showing and Hiding Levels

You can show (**expand**) or hide (**collapse**) individual levels in nested rows or columns, concealing the parts of a pivot table that you don't want to see. In a pivot table that nests Product within Category, for example, you can show only the products in a specific category and hide the rest.

To show or hide specific levels:

- Click the small triangle next to the level name in the pivot table (click again to toggle visibility). If the triangles aren't visible, choose PivotTable tab > View group > Triangles.

  or

  Double-click the cell containing the level name (double-click again to toggle visibility).

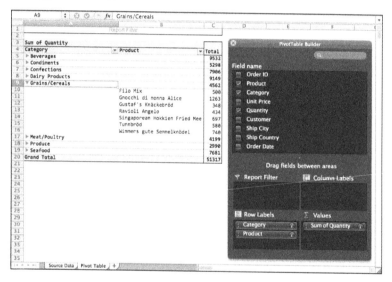

To show or hide all levels:

- In the target field, right-click any cell containing a level name and then choose Show Detail or Hide Detail from the Group and Outline submenu.

or

In the target field, select any cell containing a level name and then choose PivotTable tab > Field group > Expand or Collapse.

If you try to expand an innermost nested level, Excel opens the Show Detail dialog box listing all the fields *not* currently showing. If you select a field and then click OK, Excel adds another nested field to the pivot table.

3   Grouping Items

P ivot tables let you combine items into **groups**, which you can use to subset related values that can't be easily combined by sorting, filtering, or other means. Numbers, dates, times, and user-selected items can be grouped.

Grouping by Selected Items

To create a custom group, select the items in the pivot table that you want to group, either by clicking or dragging, and then choose Pivot-Table tab > Field group > Group button > Group Selected Items (or right-click a selected cell and then choose Group and Outline > Group from the shortcut menu).

Tip: To select adjacent cells, click the first cell and then Shift-click the last cell. To select nonadjacent cells, Command-click each cell.

For example, start with a pivot table that has these settings in the Pivot-Table Builder:

Row Labels: Ship Country
Column Labels: <empty>
Values: Quantity (summarized by Sum)
Report Filter: <empty>

In the pivot table, Command-click Canada, Mexico, and USA; right-click any selected item; and then choose Group and Outline > Group.

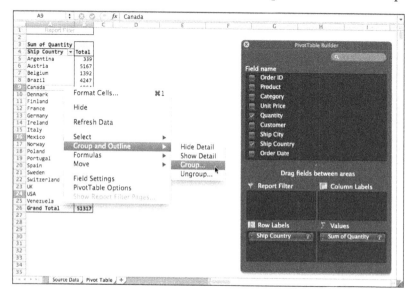

Replace the default group name (Group 1) with a meaningful name (North America). Excel also creates a new virtual field named Ship Country2 in the Row Labels box, which you can pivot on (for example, drag Ship Country2 to the Column Labels box). To remove the grouping, right-click the group name and then choose Group and Outline > Ungroup.

	A	B
A9		
1	Report Filter	
2		
3	Sum of Quantity	
4	Row Labels ▼	Total
5	▶ Argentina	339
6	▶ Austria	5167
7	▶ Belgium	1392
8	▶ Brazil	4247
9	▼ North America	
10	Canada	1984
11	Mexico	1025
12	USA	9330
13	▶ Denmark	1170
14	▶ Finland	885
15	▶ France	3254
16	▶ Germany	9213
17	▶ Ireland	1684
18	▶ Italy	822
19	▶ Norway	161
20	▶ Poland	205
21	▶ Portugal	533
22	▶ Spain	718
23	▶ Sweden	2235
24	▶ Switzerland	1275
25	▶ UK	2742
26	▶ Venezuela	2936
27	Grand Total	51317
28		

Nested Groups

You can create any number of groups and even create nested groups (groups of groups). When you create nested groups, it's usually easiest to define the broadest (outermost) group first and then progress to the innermost groups.

	A	B
1	Report Filter	
2		
3	**Sum of Quantity**	
4	Row Labels ▼	Total
5	▼ World	
6	▼ Americas	
7	▼ South America	
8	Argentina	339
9	Brazil	4247
10	Venezuela	2936
11	▼ North America	
12	Canada	1984
13	Mexico	1025
14	USA	9330
15	▼ Europe	
16	▶ Austria	5167
17	▶ Belgium	1392
18	▶ Denmark	1170
19	▶ Finland	885
20	▶ France	3254
21	▶ Germany	9213
22	▶ Ireland	1684
23	▶ Italy	822
24	▶ Norway	161
25	▶ Poland	205
26	▶ Portugal	533
27	▶ Spain	718
28	▶ Sweden	2235
29	▶ Switzerland	1275
30	▶ UK	2742
31	**Grand Total**	**51317**

Grouping by Time Periods

When a field contains dates or times, you can create groups that summarize data by time periods (hours, months, years, and so on). For example, you can use the Order Date field to summarize sales by month. Start with a pivot table that has these settings in the PivotTable Builder:

Row Labels: Order Date
Column Labels: <empty>
Values: Quantity (summarized by Sum)
Report Filter: <empty>

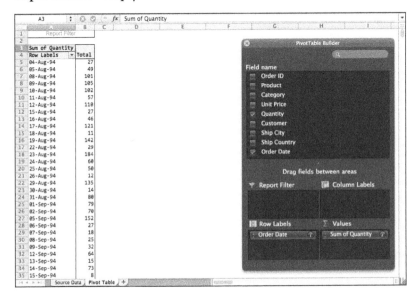

In the pivot table, right-click any cell in the Order Date (Row Labels) column and then select Group and Outline > Group from the shortcut menu. The Grouping dialog box opens. In the By list, select Months and Years (Command-click each list item to select or deselect it). Verify that the starting and ending dates are correct and then click OK.

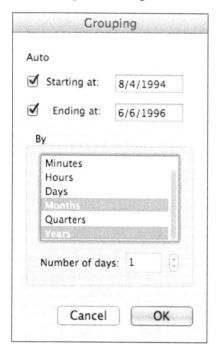

The Order Date items in the pivot table are grouped by years and by months. Excel also creates a new virtual field named Years in the Row Labels box, which you can pivot on (for example, drag Years to the Column Labels box). To remove the grouping, right-click any cell in the Order Date (Row Labels) column and then choose Group and Outline > Ungroup.

Tip: If you select only Months (and not Years) in the list box, then months in different years are combined. The Aug item, for example, would show the combined quantities for 1994 *and* 1995 (the data stop in June, 1996).

A3		
	A	**B**
1	Report Filter	
2		
3	**Sum of Quantity**	
4	Row Labels ▼	Total
5	▼ 1994	
6	Aug	1462
7	Sep	1322
8	Oct	1124
9	Nov	1669
10	Dec	1804
11	▼ 1995	
12	Jan	2200
13	Feb	1951
14	Mar	2582
15	Apr	1622
16	May	2060
17	Jun	2164
18	Jul	1635
19	Aug	2054
20	Sep	1861
21	Oct	2343
22	Nov	2657
23	Dec	1878
24	▼ 1996	
25	Jan	2682
26	Feb	3293
27	Mar	3288
28	Apr	4065
29	May	4957
30	Jun	644
31	Grand Total	51317

Grouping by Weeks

You can also group by week (or any fixed span of days). In the Grouping dialog box, select only Days (nothing else) in the By list and then type 7 in the "Number of days" box. Clear the "Starting at" checkbox and then adjust the start date to fall on the first day (typically, Sunday or Monday) of the first week of interest. If you like, adjust the end date too. Click OK. Each row in the resulting pivot table shows the start and end dates of each week.

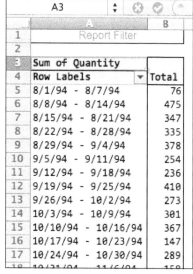

Grouping by Numbers

You can group by numbers to create a **frequency distribution**, where each entry in the pivot table contains the frequency (count) of the occurrences of values within a particular group or interval.

For example, start with a pivot table that has these settings in the Pivot-Table Builder:

Row Labels: Quantity
Column Labels: <empty>
Values: Quantity (summarized by Sum)
Report Filter: <empty>

The pivot table shows the quantity of units sold and the corresponding number of orders. The goal is to determine how many quantities are in each 10-point range (1–10, 11–20, and so on).

In the pivot table, right-click any cell in the Quantity (Row Labels) column and then select Group and Outline > Group from the shortcut menu.

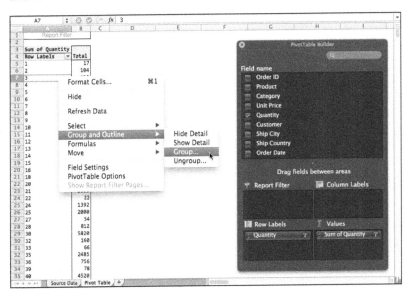

The Grouping dialog box opens. In the By box, type the size of the interval for each group (here, 10). Verify that the starting and ending points are correct and then click OK.

The Quantity items in the pivot table are grouped in uniform intervals (bins). The groups start at 1 and end at 130, in increments of 10. A column chart of a frequency distribution is a **histogram**. To remove the grouping, right-click any cell in the Quantity (Row Labels) column and then choose Group and Outline > Ungroup.

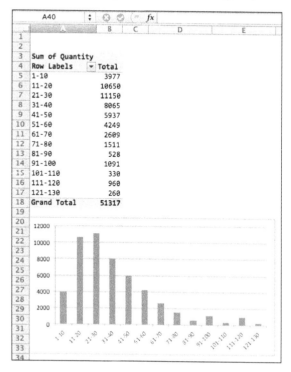

4 Calculations and Custom Formulas

When you add a field to the Values box in the PivotTable Builder, Excel (in most cases) sums all the values in that field, but you can also calculate common statistics, do multiple calculations in the same pivot table, and create custom formulas.

Calculating Common Statistics

Excel's preset calculations include common statistics: sum, count, average, maximum, percentage, rank, and so on.

To choose a preset calculation:

1 Select any cell in the pivot table.

  Excel shows the PivotTable Builder.

2 In the PivotTable Builder, click the Info button (labeled *i*) in the target field (for example, "Sum of Quantity") in the Values box. Alternatively, select any cell in the target field in the pivot table and then choose PivotTable tab > Field group > Settings.

  The PivotTable Field dialog box opens.

3 In the "Summarize by" list, choose a calculation (Sum, Count, Average,...).

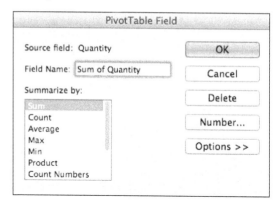

Alternatively, click the Options button to choose a more-complex calculation (difference, percentage, running total, or index).

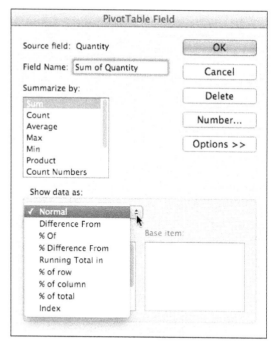

You can also change the default field name by typing a new name in the Field Name box.

4 To format the field's values, click the Number button, choose or define a new format, and then click OK.

You can change the number of decimal places, add a currency symbol, and so on.

5 Click OK to close the PivotTable Field dialog box.

Excel refreshes the pivot table with the new calculations.

Specifying Values for Empty Cells

To specify what values appear in the empty cells in a pivot table (typically, a zero, a blank, or a text indicator such as *Missing*), right-click any cell in the pivot table and then choose PivotTable Options (or choose PivotTable tab > Data group > Options). On the Display pane, enter the desired settings for the "Empty cells as" options.

Calculating Multiple Statistics

When you add multiple fields to the Values box, each field is calculated and shown in a separate column in the pivot table. To sum the Quantity and average the Unit Price, for example, drag both fields into the Values box and then follow the steps above to configure each field separately.

Similarly, you can do multiple calculations on the *same* field. To sum and average Quantity, for example, drag Quantity into the Values box twice and then configure the two Quantity fields separately.

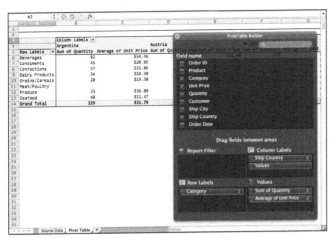

Adding Custom Calculations

In addition to choosing a preset calculation, you can define a custom **calculated field** in a pivot table.

To add a calculated field:

1 Select any cell in the pivot table.

2 Choose PivotTable tab > Field group > Formulas button > Calculated Fields. Alternatively, right-click any cell in the pivot table and then choose Formulas > Calculated Field from the shortcut menu

The Insert Calculated Field dialog box opens.

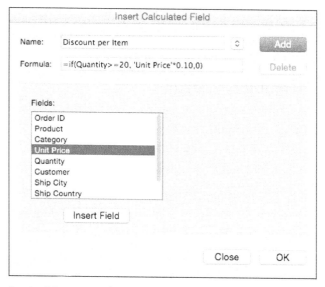

3 In the Name text box, type or paste a name for the new field.

4 In the Formula text box, enter the formula for this field.

The formula can use Excel's built-in operators and functions, or change or combine one or more of the fields in the Fields list. To insert a field name in the formula quickly, double-click the name in the list. If you manually type a field name that contains spaces or special characters, enclose the name in single quotes (for example, 'Unit Price').

5 Click OK.

In the PivotTable Builder, Excel adds the calculated field to the fields list and the Values box, so that it appears in the pivot table. Excel sums the formula for every row.

Removing a custom field from the Values box removes it from the pivot table, but it remains in the fields list for later use. To permanently delete a custom field, select it from the Name drop-down list in the Insert Calculated Field dialog box (shown above) and then click Delete.

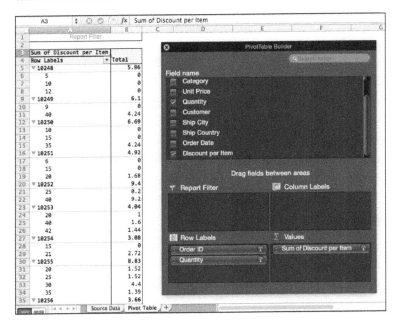

Tip: To list all calculated fields in a new worksheet, choose PivotTable tab > Field group > Formulas > List Formulas.

Troubleshooting Calculated Fields

Calculated fields have the following restrictions:

- A calculated-field formula can't refer to pivot-table grand totals or subtotals, nor can it refer to worksheet cells by address or by name.

- You can summarize a calculated field by only Sum.

- Because calculated-field formulas are always applied against the *sum* of the underlying data, Excel calculates data fields, subtotals, and grand totals before evaluating the calculated field.

In nontrivial formulas, the last restriction can cause unexpected results because the sum of products (generally) isn't equal to the product of sums. In the example above, the calculated field returns a 10 percent per-item price discount when a customer orders 20 or more units of a particular item, and no (zero) discount otherwise. In the resulting pivot table, the individual Quantity calculations are correct but the subtotals for each Order ID aren't what you'd expect (because Excel sums all an order's quantities *before* determining whether discounts apply). Another common trap: if you create a calculated field named Revenue with the formula =`'Unit Price' * Quantity`, Excel sums the prices, sums the quantities, and then multiplies the two sums—which is *not* what you want.

Sadly, there's no way to fix this problem, but there are a few (somewhat unsatisfying) workarounds for when you want sum-of-products and Excel is giving you product-of-sums:

- Add a column (field) to the underlying source data. In the sample workbook, for example, you can add a revenue formula to column J in the Source Data worksheet: type *Revenue* in cell J1, type =`D2*E2` in cell J2 (Unit Price × Quantity), and then fill down (Ctrl+D) the J2 formula to the end of the table.

- Copy (Command+C) and paste values (Option+Command+V) from the pivot table to work with independently elsewhere in the workbook.

- Write formulas outside the pivot table. See also "Controlling References to Pivot Table Cells" on page 56.

- Turn off grand totals and subtotals in the pivot table (PivotTable tab > Design group) and then calculate your own totals outside the pivot table.

5

Filtering Data

If a pivot table displays too much detail, you can **filter** (restrict) it to show only part of the source data. Excel offers two types of filtering: report filters and group filters.

Tip: If a pivot table's data source is a table (Tables tab > Table Options group > New), then any filters that you apply directly to the table have no effect on linked pivot tables. To filter data from a pivot table, you must use one of the following methods.

Report Filters

Report filters let you filter out data so that a pivot table uses only rows of interest in the source data. For example, start with a pivot table that has these settings in the PivotTable Builder:

Row Labels: Category
Column Labels: Ship City
Values: Quantity (summarized by Sum)
Report Filter: <empty>

To create a summary for only specific countries, drag the field Ship Country to the Report Filter box. The report filter field appears just above the pivot table. (If you use more than one report filter, each appears in a separate row.) To set the filter, click the drop-down arrow ▾ in the field box and then choose the countries that you want to display. To find an item, scroll the list or type the first few characters of its name in the Search box. When you're done, click ×.

Tip: To control how report filter fields are arranged in rows and columns, choose PivotTable tab > Data group > Options > Layout pane > "Report filter".

Excel uses checked items to create the pivot table, and ignores unchecked items. To quickly remove a report filter, choose the first item in the report filter list: "(Select All)" or click the Clear Filter button.

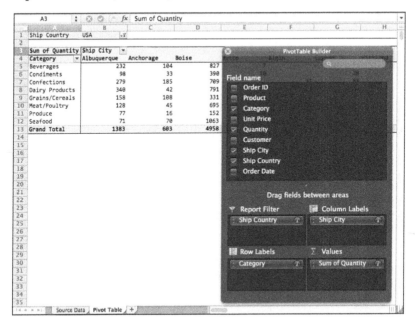

Tip: Any fields that you use for report filtering *can't* also be used for grouping (Chapter 3). For example, if you filter by Ship Country, you can't also group by Ship Country. This restriction doesn't apply to group filters (covered next).

Group Filters

Group filters—more powerful than report filters (page 46)—let you filter fields that you're using to group (Chapter 3) a pivot table to:

- Show or hide specific items (like report filters, except that you can't create report filters for grouping fields).

- Create complex conditions that subset data. For example, you can show or hide dates that fall in a specific time period or names that begin or end with a certain letter.

- Filter on multiple fields and configure them independently (Excel **additively** applies every filter at the same time).

The examples in this section use a pivot table with the following settings in the PivotTable Builder:

Row Labels: Category, Product
Column Labels: Ship Country
Values: Quantity (summarized by Sum)
Report Filter: <empty>

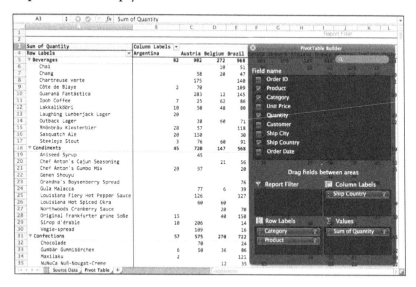

To create a group filter:

1 Click the drop-down arrow ▾ to the right of a Row Labels or Column Labels cell.

   The filter list opens.

2 If you're grouping on multiple fields, choose a field from the "Select field" drop-down list at top.

3   Set the desired options in the filter list and then click OK.

To show or hide specific items, select or clear their checkboxes. To find an item, scroll the list or type the first few characters of its name in the Search box.

To show or hide items that contain specific text, begin or end with a certain letter, and so on, choose an option from the "By label" menu. For example, to show only items that begin with "U", choose Begins With and then type *U* in the text box that appears.

To show or hide calculated values based on numerical criteria (less than, greater than, Top 10, and so on), choose an option from the "By value" menu. For example, to show only items less than 500, choose Less Than and then type *500* in the text box that appears.

To sort items, click Ascending or Descending. To use a custom sort order, choose PivotTable tab > Data group > Options > Layout pane > Sort.

To remove a filter (show everything for the field), click the Clear Filter button. If you have multiple filters, you must remove each one separately.

4 To filter by other grouping fields, repeat the preceding steps for each row label or column label.

Filtering Nested Fields

Label filters and value filters can get tricky when you work with nested fields (Chapter 2). For example, the effect of the By Value > Less Than > 500 command differs depending on whether you apply it to the Product or Category field (recall that Product is nested within Category in this example). Applied to Product, the pivot table shows products that sold fewer than 500 units (as you'd expect). Applied to Category, only categories with sales fewer than 500 units across *all* their products appear. Because every category has sales greater than 500 units in the current example, the filter hides every category and shows an empty pivot table (which is correct logically but might not be what you'd expect).

Note that if you apply a filter to a row field (Category or Products, in this example), your column fields (Ship Country) have no effect. Likewise, row filters don't affect column filters.

6 Tricks with Pivot Tables

Excel's arsenal of pivot-table features offers a few nonobvious ways to solve common problems.

Creating a Frequency Tabulation

You can use a pivot table to quickly create a frequency tabulation for a single column of data. For example, in the sample workbook (page 1), switch to the Source Data worksheet, select the Ship Country column (click the H column heading), choose Data tab > Analysis group > PivotTable arrow > Create Manual PivotTable, and then create the pivot table (page 4). In the PivotTable Builder, drag the Ship Country field into the Row Labels box and then drag it again into the Values box. The resulting pivot table tallies the number of times that each country appears in the column. You can group, filter, and chart this tabulation as you would any pivot table. See also "Grouping by Numbers" on page 35.

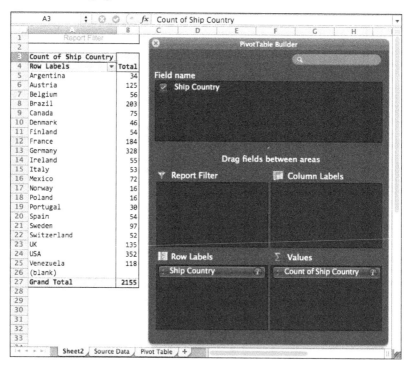

Unlinking a Pivot Table from its Source Data

Excel doesn't provide a direct way to "unlink" a pivot table from its source data, but you can create an unlinked copy of a pivot table in a few steps (handy if you want to send someone a pivot table summary report but not its underlying data).

To create an unlinked copy of a pivot table:

1 Select the entire pivot table.

   To select the entire pivot table, drag to select all the pivot table's cells (including headers) or right-click any cell in the pivot table and then choose Select > Entire Table. Alternatively, click anywhere in the pivot table and then choose PivotTable tab > Data group > Select > Entire Table.

2 Choose View > Scrapbook.

   The Scrapbook window appears.

3 In the Scrapbook window, click the small arrow next to the Add button and then choose Add Selection.

4 Activate the Excel worksheet (the entire pivot table should still be selected) and then choose Edit > Clear > All.

   Excel erases the pivot table.

5 In the Scrapbook window, click the Paste button.

   Excel pastes the values and formatting of the original pivot table, unlinked from the source data. You can close the Scrapbook window.

Controlling References to Pivot Table Cells

If you create a formula that refers to a cell within a pivot table, use the GETPIVOTDATA function, which ensures that formulas still return the correct results even if you rearrange the pivot table (page 8).

```
GETPIVOTDATA(pivot_table, name)
```

The *pivot_table* argument refers to the target pivot table and can be a cell or range of cells in the pivot table, a named range that contains the pivot table, or a label stored in a cell above the pivot table. It's generally safest to set *pivot_table* to the cell at the top left corner of the target pivot table, which stays anchored in place even when the pivot table is updated or rearranged. If *pivot_table* spans a range that contains multiple pivot tables (not recommended), then GETPIVOTDATA retrieves a value from whichever pivot table was created most recently in that range.

The *name* argument is a quote-enclosed string that describes the cell in *pivot_table* that contains the value to return, provided that value is visible in *pivot_table*.

For example, consider a pivot table with the settings:

Row Labels: Category
Column Labels: Ship Country
Values: Quantity (summarized by Sum)
Report Filter: <empty>

The formula:

```
=GETPIVOTDATA($A$3, "Argentina Beverages")
```

returns 82, and:

```
=GETPIVOTDATA($A$3, "Condiments Austria")
```

returns 720.

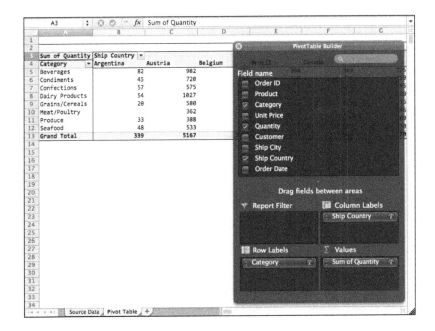

The formula:

    =GETPIVOTDATA(A3, "Argentina")

returns 339 (the grand total for Argentina), and:

    =GETPIVOTDATA(A3, "Condiments")

returns 5298 (the grand total for Condiments).

Rearranging the pivot table doesn't affect the results; the preceding formulas would still return the same values if you dragged Category to Column Labels or dragged Ship Country to Row Labels.

The formula:

    =GETPIVOTDATA(A3, "Argentina Fruit")

returns the error value #N/A because Fruit is not a valid Category value.

If you filter (Chapter 5) the pivot table to hide Argentina or Beverages, then the formula:

    =GETPIVOTDATA(A3, "Argentina Beverages")

returns the error value #REF!.

Index